PYTHONS

Serena Stone

The World of Snakes

www.av2books.com

Step 1
Go to **www.av2books.com**

Step 2
Enter this unique code
LUSIWJ3XG

Step 3
Explore your interactive eBook!

AV2 is optimized for use on any device

Your interactive eBook comes with...

Contents
Browse a live contents page to easily navigate through resources

Audio
Listen to sections of the book read aloud

Videos
Watch informative video clips

Weblinks
Gain additional information for research

Slideshows
View images and captions

Try This!
Complete activities and hands-on experiments

Key Words
Study vocabulary, and complete a matching word activity

Quizzes
Test your knowledge

Share
Share titles within your Learning Management System (LMS) or Library Circulation System

Citation
Create bibliographical references following the Chicago Manual of Style

This title is part of our AV2 digital subscription

1-Year 3–8 Subscription
ISBN 978-1-7911-3306-1

Access hundreds of AV2 titles with our digital subscription.
Sign up for a FREE trial at **www.av2books.com/trial**

PYTHONS

CONTENTS

Long and Strong

Pythons are a group of snakes known for their size and strength. This group includes some of the longest snakes in the world. Python bites can be very serious. A python's sharp teeth dig deep. However, pythons do not use **venom** to hunt their **prey**. Instead, they **constrict** their food. Pythons are old world snakes. This means that python **species** are not found naturally in the Americas.

WARNING

Some large pythons are considered dangerous to humans. However, most people can run much more quickly than pythons can move.

Pythons are **reptiles**. Like other reptiles, they are cold-blooded creatures that have backbones. Their skin is covered with scales.

SNAKE BITES

The **smallest python**, the **anthill python**, grows about **24 inches** (61 centimeters) long.

There are **41 species** of python in the world.

What Do Pythons Look Like?

Pythons can range from a few feet long to up to nearly the length of a bus. They are considered heavy, bulky snakes for their size. The largest python is the **reticulated** python. These pythons may grow more than 30 feet (9 meters) long.

Measuring Up

Average snake lengths

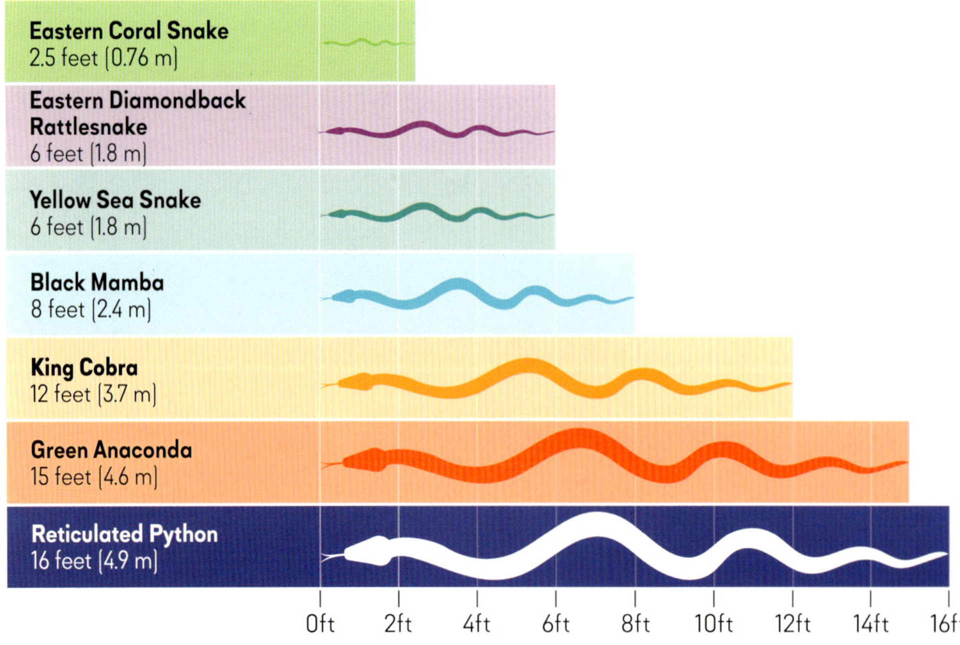

Most pythons are brightly colored. Different pythons have different patterns on their bodies. Some have stripes or **blotches**, while others have patterns that look like large nets or diamond shapes.

Pythons come in many colors, including green, silver-gray, and black. Some even change color as they age. Green and brown are common colors that **camouflage** pythons in their surroundings.

The Life Cycle

Like all living things, pythons have a life cycle. A python will be born, grow, and **reproduce**. It may live more than 30 years.

Pythons reproduce by laying eggs. The number of eggs laid at a time ranges from about 5 to more than 100.

2

Many python mothers guard their eggs until they hatch after about two months. Pythons wrap themselves around their eggs to keep them warm and safe.

Baby pythons are called hatchlings. They hunt for food such as small mice, rats, or birds. Pythons grow to adult size after about one to five years.

3

4

Adult male pythons travel to find a mate. They do this by following scent trails left by females. Some male pythons will fight each other over a mate.

A Python's Body

Like all living things, a python has many different **adaptations**. Some keep the snake safe. Others help it to survive in its **habitat**.

Tongue
Like other snakes, pythons use their **forked** tongues to smell. This helps them track down their prey.

Pits
Most pythons have heat-sensitive areas called pits near their mouths. Pits help a python find where its prey is hiding.

Skin

Pythons shed their skin as they grow. A python rubs its head against rough objects until the skin comes loose.

Head

A python's head is shaped like a long triangle. The snake's teeth are curved backward to help it grab its prey.

Where Pythons Live

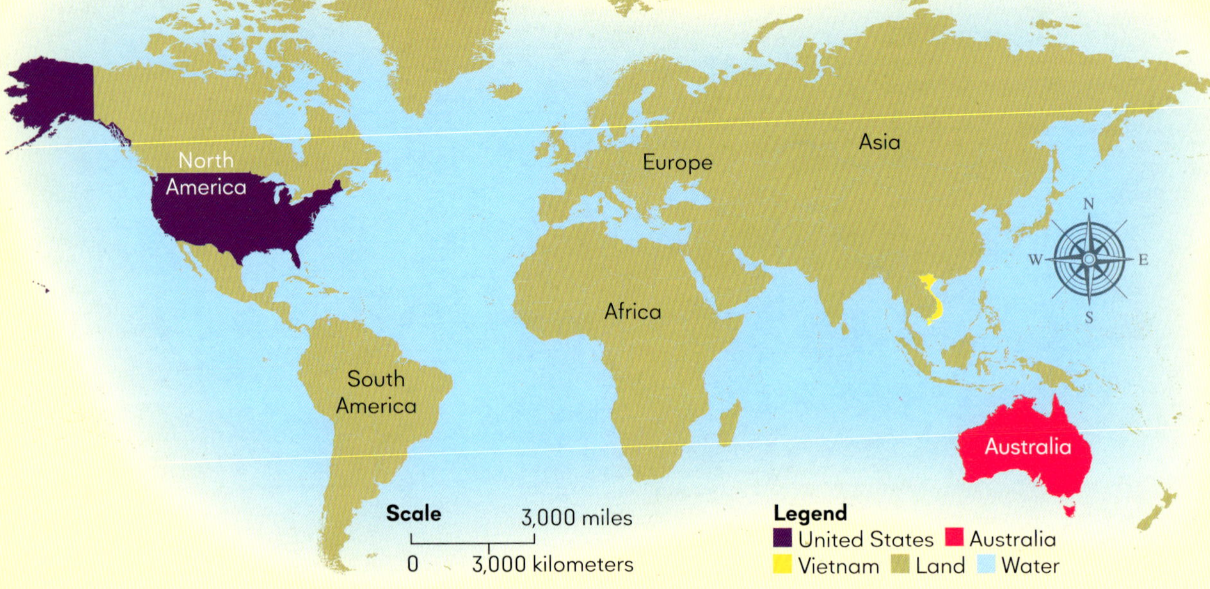

Pythons mainly live in Asia, Africa, Australia, and islands in the South Pacific. Some have been introduced to other continents. Pythons live in rainforests and swamps. Some also live in drier places, such as grasslands or woodlands.

Python Range

Africa

Asia

Australia

Python Habitats

Desert

Forest

Grassland

Rainforest

Wetland

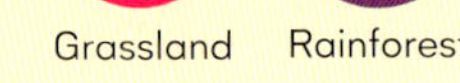

Burmese Python

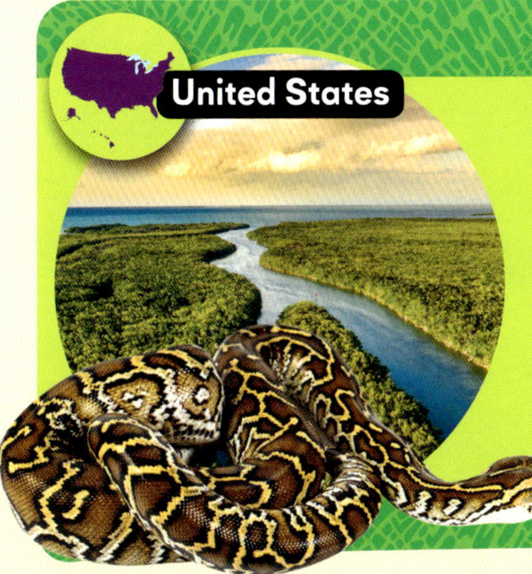

The Burmese python is from Southeast Asia. However, it has been introduced to other countries. This snake is now an **invasive species** in the **Florida Everglades**. Burmese pythons are gray or tan, with reddish to dark brown-black blotches. These snakes can stay underwater for up to 30 minutes.

Green Tree Python

This brightly colored python is found in rainforests in New Guinea, Indonesia, and northern Australia. Green tree pythons live in trees. When born, they are yellow or orange. They turn green as they grow. This color helps the pythons hide in trees. They mostly eat lizards, bats, and small rodents. Green tree pythons are often confused with the unrelated emerald tree boas.

Reticulated Python

Vietnam

This colorful snake lives mainly in Southeast Asia and on South Pacific islands. It gets its name from the marks on its body, which form a net- or diamond-shaped pattern. Reticulated pythons are often found in rainforests, wetlands, and woodlands. Their prey ranges in size from bats to bears.

On the Hunt

Pythons hunt during the day or at night. They can eat almost any animal that will fit into their bodies. Pythons hunt by ambushing prey. A python sits and waits for an animal to come near, then strikes. Some python species hide in shallow water to hunt.

If a python eats a very large animal, it may not have to eat again for months or even a year.

To catch its food, a python grabs its prey with its sharp teeth. Then, the snake wraps itself around the prey and squeezes tightly to crush it. A python swallows its meals headfirst.

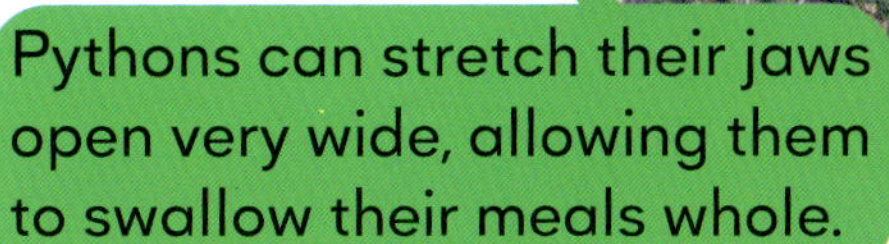

Pythons can stretch their jaws open very wide, allowing them to swallow their meals whole.

Keeping Safe

Pythons are not very fast snakes, so escaping from danger can be difficult for them. Many pythons keep safe by hiding. Their camouflage lets them hide from danger. Some pythons keep safe by hiding in burrows dug by other animals.

Other pythons will play dead to look less appetizing. A ball or royal python will curl into a ball with its head in the center for protection. If cornered, a python may fight back. It will strike at a **predator** and try to constrict it.

Because of its rounded head, the black-headed python is one of the few pythons that can dig its own burrow.

Young pythons may be hunted by birds, wild dogs, large frogs, insects, and even other snakes. Large adult pythons are too big for most animals to eat.

Threats to Pythons

The biggest threats to large pythons are people. People hunt pythons and other large snakes for their skins. The skins are then sold for meat, or for clothing items such as purses, cowboy boots, and shoes.

Many pythons are now losing their homes because of logging, farming, and ranching. People have cleared forests in many areas where the snakes used to live. This loss of habitat can make it hard for pythons to find food and shelter.

In Australia, it is against the law to collect green tree pythons from nature for the pet trade.

Some people see pythons as threats or pests. They may kill these snakes out of fear. Others take pythons from nature as pets. When this happens, it can cause their numbers to drop. Escaped pet pythons can become invasive species, posing a danger to animals in their new home as well.

Today, there may be as many as 300,000 Burmese pythons in Florida.

Several species of pythons are considered vulnerable or **endangered** in their native habitats. In many countries around the world, laws are being made to protect snakes and make sure they do not die out.

SNAKE BITES

Globally, **Burmese python** numbers dropped **30 percent** between **2007** and **2017**.

Australia's Ramsay's python was **removed from the endangered species list** in **2017**.

ACTIVITY
Create a Snake

There are many different kinds of snakes in the world. They all have certain features in common. However, each snake also has its own unique features. They help the snake live in its home.

Make your own snake by answering the following questions:

1. What is your snake called?
2. Where does it live?
3. What features does it share with other snakes?
4. What features help it live in its home? How do these features do this?
5. What does your snake look like?
6. Use a pencil or pen to draw your snake living in its home. Make sure to include all of its features.

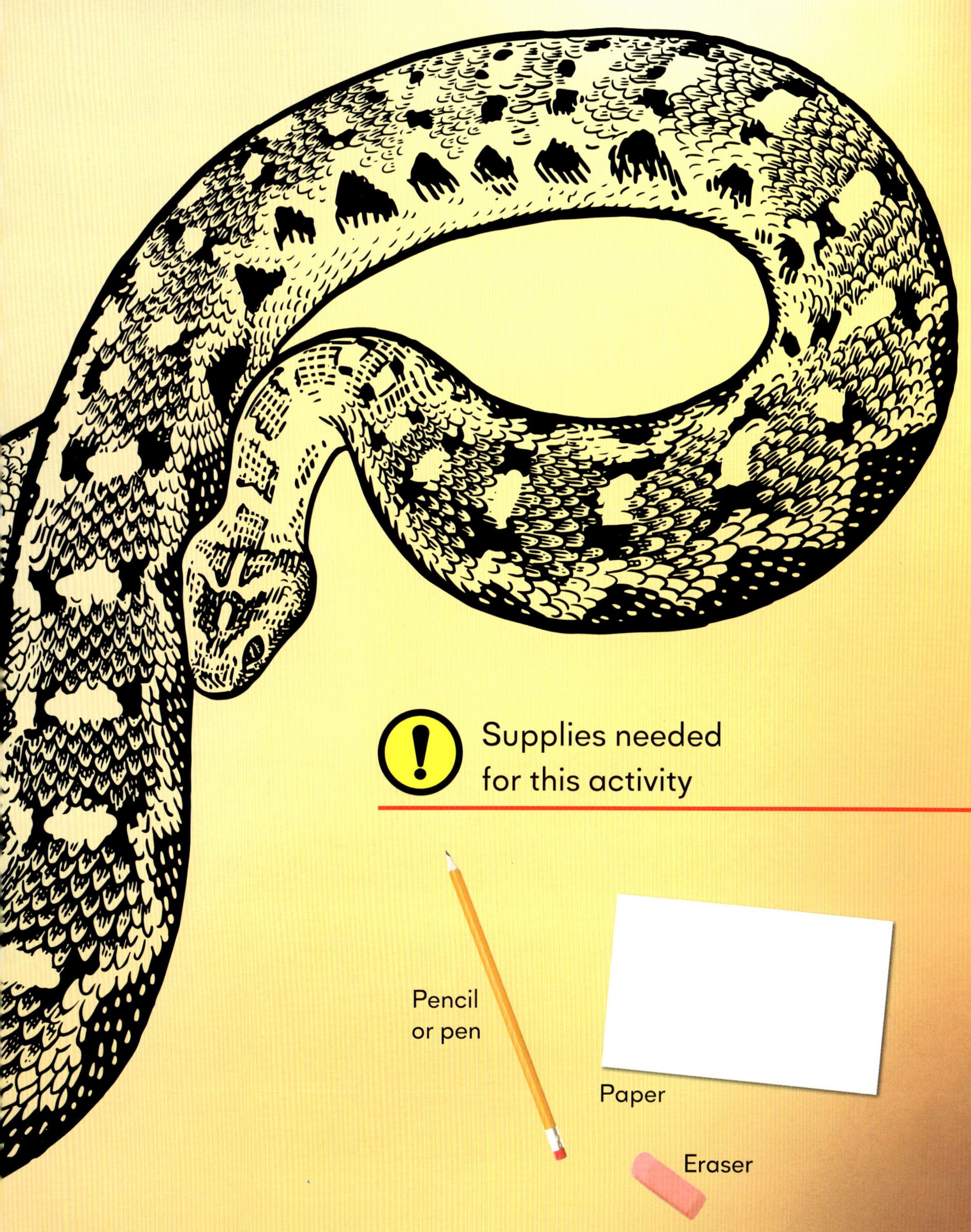

Supplies needed for this activity

PYTHON QUIZ

How well do you know your pythons? Take this short quiz to find out.

1 What is the largest python species?

2 How many python species are there?

3 How do pythons reproduce?

4 What are a python's colors and patterns often used for?

5 What shape are the marks on a reticulated python?

6 What are the pits on a python's face used for?

7 About how long is the shortest python?

8 In what direction do pythons swallow their prey?

ANSWERS

1. The reticulated python **2.** 41 **3.** By laying eggs **4.** Camouflage **5.** Net- or diamond-shaped **6.** To find prey **7.** 24 inches (61 cm) **8.** Headfirst

Key Words

adaptations: changes in animals or plants that make them better able to survive in their homes

blotches: marks not regular in shape

camouflage: a natural disguise

constrict: tighten around something

endangered: close to becoming extinct

Florida Everglades: huge wetlands in the southern part of Florida

forked: one end divided into two, like the shape of the letter "Y"

habitat: the place where a plant or animal lives

invasive species: a species that has been introduced to a new home and is harming the plants and animals in the area

predator: an animal that hunts other animals

prey: animals that are hunted by other animals

reproduce: to have babies

reptiles: cold-blooded animals that are usually covered with scales

reticulated: marked with a net or diamond pattern that has many small sections

species: a group of closely related animals or plants

venom: a poisonous chemical produced by some animals

Index

Get the best of both worlds.

AV2 bridges the gap between print and digital.

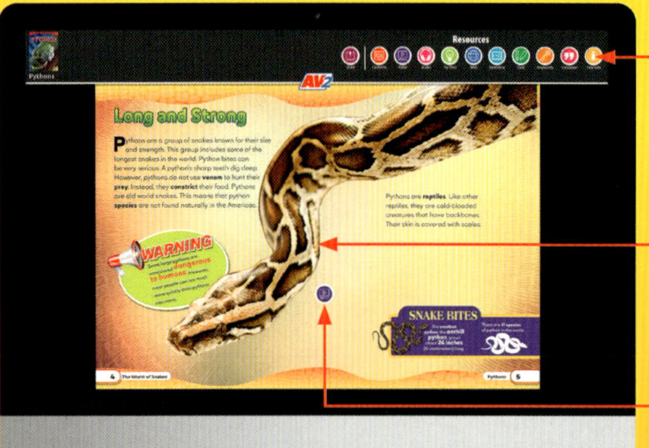

The expandable resources toolbar enables quick access to content including **videos**, **audio**, **activities**, **weblinks**, **slideshows**, **quizzes**, and **key words**.

Animated videos make static images come alive.

Resource icons on each page help readers to further **explore key concepts**.

Published by AV2
276 5th Avenue
Suite 704 #917
New York, NY 10001
Website: www.av2books.com

Library of Congress Control Number: 2021940097

ISBN 978-1-7911-4157-8 (hardcover)
ISBN 978-1-7911-4158-5 (softcover)
ISBN 978-1-7911-4159-2 (multi-user eBook)

Printed in Guangzhou, China
1 2 3 4 5 6 7 8 9 0 25 24 23 22 21

062021
101120

Art Director: Terry Paulhus Project Coordinator: John Willis

Every reasonable effort has been made to trace ownership and to obtain permission to reprint copyright material. The publisher would be pleased to have any errors or omissions brought to its attention so that they may be corrected in subsequent printings.

The publisher acknowledges Alamy, Getty Images, Minden Pictures, Shutterstock, and Wikimedia as the primary image suppliers for this title.

View new titles and product videos at www.av2books.com